Keys to Raising Children with Autism

A GUIDE ON HOW TO HANDLE CHILDREN WITH AUTISM

Carolyn Lamb

Table of contents

Chapter 1:Learning about Autism Spectrum Disorder

ASD, or autism spectrum disorder, is a developmental disease characterized by restricted communication, behavioral difficulties, and a narrow range of interests and activities. In the United States, it is thought to affect 1 in 44 children aged 8 and younger, and it is more frequent in males than in girls.

ASD sufferers may exhibit a broad range of behavioral symptoms, from a failure to establish healthy peer connections to a delay in or complete absence of spoken language. For those who do talk, there may be a delay in their capacity to carry on a discussion with others or repeated use of words. Temper tantrums, impulsivity, aggression, hyperactivity, lack of focus, and short attention span are further signs of autism.

Evidence-based autism therapy encourages the growth of social and communicative abilities while reducing behaviors that hinder functional and academic progress. Intensive, ongoing, evidence-based autism therapy may improve a person's capacity to learn, communicate, participate in society, and reach their full potential. For the categorization and diagnosis of ASD, the Diagnostic and Statistical Manual of Mental Disorders is the most extensively used resource. The diagnostic criteria for

ASD, which were formerly thought of as three separate diagnoses (namely, autistic disorder, pervasive developmental disorder—not otherwise specified, and Asperger's disorder), were reinterpreted in the most current version (DSM-5; American Psychiatric Association, 2013). However, the DSM-5 categorizes ASD as a single disease that includes constrained, repetitive patterns of behavior, interests, or activities in addition to persistent difficulties in social communication and social interaction.

A developmental impairment known as an autism spectrum disorder (ASD) may have an impact on a child's behavior, speech, and social skills. You may not notice delays in social and communicative skills during the first year of life since the majority of children with ASD will sit, crawl, and walk on time.

Its manifestation differs from person to person, but it generally impacts a child's ability to communicate and connect socially with their parents, classmates, and/or instructors. Additionally, it affects how the youngster thinks and acts. They may engage in repetitious or strange play, behavior, and thought patterns as a result of it.

ASD is often diagnosed in the early years of children and may have long-term implications. According to recent studies, males are diagnosed with ASD three times more often than girls, although additional study is required to fully explain this gender disparity.

The primary traits of autism spectrum disorder may be divided into two groups:

1. Difficulties navigating our social environment: Kids with ASD vary in how they approach or react to social encounters. Without making eye contact or engaging in physical touch, children may try to connect with others. Some people may find conversations and play difficult or include subjects that are of great importance to them. It may be challenging to grasp the sophisticated language, nuanced social conventions, and nonverbal communication (such as gestures and facial expressions). They can find it difficult or frustrating to establish and maintain connections.

2. Repetitive movements, actions, or interests: Children with ASD often engage in repetitive activities such as flapping their hands or repeating certain noises or phrases. They could be very passionate about a certain subject, making it challenging to participate in other activities. They could like patterns and become upset when such habits are interrupted. They might overreact or underreact to sensory input.

The amount of assistance required might vary greatly. Some kids and adults with ASD can carry out all of the regular everyday tasks. Others need strong support networks for the duration of their life. Individualized supports and environmental modifications that maximize inclusion possibilities and offer the person with ASD the greatest chance of success may need to be developed by caregivers, service providers, and community members.

The first step in assisting a kid who has autism and similar illnesses is recognizing their existence.

It's common for kids with autism spectrum disorders to have trouble processing sensory data. Things they see, taste, or touch may cause them to respond more powerfully. They could have a hard time ignoring or adapting to things like noises and odors. Their oral, fine motor and gross motor abilities often lag. These challenges delay their ability to interpret social information.

Children with autism spectrum conditions thus often shy away from the challenging linguistic and social environment. They instead look toward the world of things. Things like video games and television are far less complicated and hence enticing and even comforting to kids with an autism spectrum disorder.

To navigate what they perceive to be a complicated environment, children with autism spectrum disorder frequently create simplification methods. These tactics often take the form of constrained, recurring patterns of behavior, interests, and activities.

Researchers have discovered around 10 distinct genes that, when combined in various ways, cause disorders that are collectively referred to as autism spectrum disorder. Children on the spectrum themselves might vary greatly. Each individual has unique talents and shortcomings.

Chapter 2 : ASD's Early Warning Signs and Symptoms

Developmental impairment known as an autism spectrum disorder (ASD) is brought on by variations in the brain. People with ASD may struggle with confined or repetitive activities or interests, as well as social communication and engagement. Additionally, people with ASD may learn, move, or pay attention in various ways. It is crucial to remember that some individuals without ASD may also experience some of these symptoms. However, these traits may make life extremely difficult for those with ASD.

Social Interaction and Communication Skills

For those with ASD, developing social communication and interpersonal skills might be difficult. Examples of social interaction and communication traits connected to ASD include:

1. eschews or breaks eye contact
2. does not react to name by the age of nine months
3. does not display joyful, sad, angry, or astonished facial emotions by the age of nine months.
4. not engaging in basic interactive games like pat-a-cake by the age of 12 months

5. By the age of one year, makes little or no gestures (for example, does not wave goodbye)
6. at the age of 15 months, does not share interests with others (for example, shows you an object that they like)
7. at the age of 18 months, does not point to show you anything intriguing.
8. at the age of 24 months, can not recognize when others are harmed or unhappy.
9. at the age of 36 months, does not observe or engage in play with other children.
10. at the age of 48 months, does not pretend to be someone else during play, such as a teacher or a superhero.
11. not perform for you in song, dance, or acting by the age of 60 months

Behaviors or Interests that are Restricted or Repetitive

People with ASD can exhibit peculiar habits or hobbies. ASD differs from disorders that are solely characterized by issues with social interaction and communication under these behaviors or interests.

Examples of limited or repetitive ASD-related activities and interests include:

1. Child playing on the carpet with toy blocks in close-up.

2. sets toys or other items in a line and becomes irate if the order is altered.
3. repeatedly uses the same words or phrases (called echolalia)
4. uses the same playstyle with toys every time.
5. is focused on object components (for example, wheels)
6. disturbed by even little changes
7. possesses obsessions
8. must adhere to specified procedures
9. Has unexpected responses to sounds, smells, tastes, sights, or feelings. Flaps hands, rocks body, or spins around.

Most persons with ASD also exhibit other similar traits.
These might consist of:

- delayed linguistic abilities
- talents for moving slowly
- delayed abilities in learning or thinking
- Inattentive, impulsive, or hyperactive behavior
- a seizure or epilepsy condition
- unusual patterns of eating and sleeping
- digestive disorders (for example, constipation)
- unusual emotional or mood swings
- excessive concern, tension, or anxiety

Lack of fear or unexpectedly high levels of fear

It's crucial to remember that children with ASD may not exhibit all of the behaviors that are shown below as examples.

1. You must comprehend the many varieties of autism and the symptoms that each one presents if your kid has autism.
2. Your efforts to assist your kid deal with the disease will be guided by your knowledge of the particular difficulties each form of autism presents.

Asperger's syndrome, Rett syndrome, childhood disintegrative disorder, Kanner's syndrome, and pervasive developmental disorder-not otherwise specified are the five main kinds of autism.

1. **Autism Spectrum Disorder**

Before 2013, the term "Asperger's syndrome" was widely used, however now, doctors no longer refer to it by that name. The DSM-5 diagnostic handbook later classed it as level 1 autism spectrum disorder. However, Asperger's syndrome is sometimes used informally; in fact, it is more often used in autistic groups than in level 1 spectrum conditions.

A kid with level 1 autism spectrum condition will be intelligent and verbally skilled above normal, but they will struggle with social communication. A kid with level 1 autism spectrum condition will often exhibit the symptoms listed below:

1. The rigidity of thinking and action
2. Moving between tasks might be difficult
3. issues with executive functioning
4. Lack of emotional expression in their voice, flat monotonous speech, or changing their pitch to match their surroundings
5. Interaction challenges with classmates in school or at home

2.**Syndrome Rett**

A rare neurodevelopmental disease called Rett syndrome is first identified in infants. Despite being more common in females, the illness may still be identified in boys. A kid with Rett syndrome has difficulties that touch practically every part of their daily lives. The good news is that, with the right care, your kid may still have a fun and full life. You may spend time as a family and provide encouragement so that the youngster can pursue their interests.

Rett syndrome symptoms often include:

1. Loss of coordination and regular movement
2. Communication and speech difficulties
3. Breathing issues sometimes

3. **Child Destructive Disorder (CDD)**

A neurodevelopmental illness called childhood disintegrative disorder (CDD) commonly referred to as Heller's syndrome or disintegrative psychosis is characterized by the delayed onset of developmental issues with language, motor abilities, or social function. A youngster enjoys typical growth in these areas before hitting a wall between the ages of three and ten. For parents who were unaware that their kid had autism issues all along, the loss of developmental progress may be very upsetting.

Though experts have connected CDD to the neurobiology of the brain, the exact reason is uncertain. Boy patients with childhood disintegrative disorder are more prevalent. Only one female will experience the disease out of every 10 instances, with nine males.

In CDD, regressions in more than two developmental areas of the kid's life start to occur unexpectedly after the youngster has had normal development up to the disorder's onset.

Any of the following talents and abilities might be lost by the child:

1. If toileting abilities were already developed
2. Acquired vocabulary or language
3. Social abilities and adaptable actions
4. A few motor abilities

4. **The Kanner Syndrome**

Leo Kanner, a psychiatrist at John Hopkins University, first identified Kanner's condition as infantile autism in 1943. The illness is also referred to by doctors as a classic autistic disorder. Children that have Kanner's syndrome will seem beautiful, awake, and clever while also having the following disorder-specific traits:

1. Absence of emotional ties to others
2. Challenges in connection and communication
3. An obsession with manipulating items and uncontrolled speaking
4. a strong rote memory and visuospatial abilities with significant learning challenges in other areas

5. **No Other Specified Pervasive Developmental Disorder (PDD-NOS)**

A moderate form of autism known as Pervasive Developmental Disorder - Not Otherwise Specified (PDD-NOS) manifests a variety of symptoms. The most typical signs are difficulties with language and social development.

Language, walking, and other motor skill development delays may occur in your kid. By studying the kid and observing the areas in which the youngster shows a weakness, such as interacting with others, you may determine this sort of autism. PDD-NOS, which is a term used to describe someone who has some symptoms but not all of them, is also frequently referred to as "subthreshold autism."

Chapter 3 : Autism-related Misconceptions

Our community must be aware of and work to dispel prevalent misunderstandings regarding autism.

Below, these widespread misunderstandings are examined.

1.Autism is a condition

Frequently asked, is autism an illness?

Actually, autism is a developmental condition, which is the reality. NOT an illness, it is. An individual's cognitive, emotional, and social abilities are affected by autism, a spectrum condition.

ASD may manifest in a person as a mix of distinctive cognitive and behavioral characteristics.

2.There is a treatment for autism.

Is autism treatable? Is there a cure for this spectrum condition that is perfect? It's one of the most common inquiries concerning ASD.

In actuality, there is no treatment for ASD since it is a developmental issue and not an illness. A person with an autism spectrum condition may benefit from speech therapy, play therapy, and behavioral treatment to lessen the negative effects of the disease on their lives.

The person may learn adaptable skills required for everyday living. They could learn how to control their conduct and emotions as well as participate in social interactions.

3.: Vaccines may lead to autism

Can vaccinations lead to autism?

Truth: According to research, a combination of hereditary and environmental factors may cause autism. Immunity against illnesses like measles, tetanus, and rabies that are avoidable is provided through vaccinations.

Many studies have attempted and failed to draw a connection between vaccination and autism.

No component of vaccination may change a child's or an adult's genetic composition. No vaccines can result in autism.

4.All autistic people are geniuses.

True: There are several symptoms associated with an autism spectrum disorder. The intensity of these symptoms varies from person to person.

A keen interest in a specific subject or area is a typical ASD sign. That may make a youngster or adult very good at drawing, painting, taking photos, writing code, or playing music. However, only around 10% of all autistic people possess these savant abilities.

5. Autism is intellectual impairment.

The truth is that autistic children are special. They use many "languages" to communicate their requirements, wants, and feelings. We sometimes struggle to comprehend their distinctive modes of expression. They don't necessarily have an intellectual deficiency, however.

The many forms of intelligence in autistic children cannot be measured using traditional IQ testing. Speak with an SLP or an autism specialist if you are unsure about your child's intellectual capacity.

6.People with autism are not emotional

Truth: People with autism are capable of experiencing all types of emotions. Without autism, every person has unique methods of expressing the same feeling. Each emotion may be expressed in a non-traditional way by someone with a certain set of behavioral features.

ASD sufferers have social communication disorders (SCD). As a result, it is typical for people with autism to struggle with identifying and reacting to other people's emotions. Just like everyone else, they could experience happiness, grief, rage, frustration, and embarrassment. They find it challenging to communicate these feelings traditionally, however.

7.All individuals with autism have learning difficulties

Truth: Everybody learns differently. Some people study by reading. Videos may be used by some to learn. Others could gain knowledge by listening.

A person with autism could have a distinct learning style that differs from the conventional educational model. Many kids who are diagnosed with ASD need special schooling. Others, on the other hand, may just need a few sessions of play therapy, behavior therapy, or speech therapy before they start going to regular school. Professional speech therapy might assist if your kid with ASD is having difficulties in the classroom.

8. Poor parenting causes autism.

Truth: The "refrigerator mother theory" gained traction in the 1940s. It claimed that autism is brought on by parental coldness or lack of warmth. The founder and head of the Autism Research Institute, Bernard Rimland, refuted this hypothesis, nevertheless.

Ineffective parenting may increase a child's chance of developing their own interpersonal issues, anxiety, anger, and depression. But it doesn't result in autistic spectrum disorder (ASD).

9. Kids with autism may "grow out" of it

Truth: Since autism is categorized as a "developmental condition," many people mistakenly think that children outgrow it. Autism is a chronic condition. The signs of ASD cannot be "overcome" by children on their own.

For a kid with ASD, early treatments are usually important to lessen their symptoms and overall effects. To combat the effects of social communication problems in children, counseling is nearly always required (SCD).

10.Autism may be cured with special diets

Can certain foods treat autism?

The truth is that there is no connection between food and autism. Autism cannot be cured by food.

Autism-affected children often have a predilection for certain foods. They could have a strong dislike for items that have a particular color or texture. They're often referred to as "picky eaters."

If your kid exhibits a fondness for or aversion to a certain meal, see a nutritionist put up a well-balanced diet using the foods they appreciate.

11. Autism is on the rise.

The fact is that autism has existed for a long time. It has always been as widespread as it is now. Better procedures and instruments are now available for diagnosing autism spectrum disorder in youngsters (ASD). Resources and knowledge about ASD have grown throughout time.

The resources enable us to develop a thorough diagnostic quickly. As a consequence, 1 in 68 kids in the US now has an ASD diagnosis. As a consequence, many kids with ASD are getting the early attention, encouragement, and treatment they need.

12. Autism exclusively affects nonverbal people

Truth: Several autistic people have excellent functioning. Researchers, academicians, educators, performers such as singers and musicians, and composers may all be autistic.

A youngster may not talk if the signs of autism spectrum disorder are severe. Speech therapy for non-verbal ASD may help a kid express themselves in these situations. A very young, non-speaking youngster who receives speech therapy sometimes develops some speech. In other situations, the speech therapist instructs the young patient to utilize supplementary and alternate modes of communication (AAC).

A youngster may "talk" via sign language, graphic boards, computers, or any combination of these.

13. People with autism are violent

Truth: Children with autism spectrum disorders may sometimes find it difficult when they are unable to communicate. Additionally, they could be overly sensitive to certain aromas, noises, and textures.

Children with ASD often dislike changes in their surroundings and daily schedule.
Outbursts may be brought on by exposure to "upsetting" settings. These are sometimes mistaken for "temper tantrums" by parents and spectators. The way your kid is attempting to communicate their discomfort to you, however, is what matters.

Consult a behaviorist to determine the appropriate action to take in certain circumstances. In most cases, relaxing the kid involves addressing the causes of sensory overload or mental discomfort.

14.Autism is a mental health issue

The fact is that autism is NOT a mental health condition. It is of the neuro-developmental kind. Numerous investigations on people with ASD have shown abnormal neurotransmitter patterns and brain architecture.
But everyone with autism is more susceptible to subsequently experiencing a mental health problem. The most prevalent mental health issues among people with ASD include conduct disorder, anxiety, depression, and ADHD.

15. People with autism are reluctant to build social connections.

People with ASD indeed have trouble making new friends. History, however, demonstrates that many people with ASD form intimate bonds, find love, and eventually have families of their own.

They could each have unique methods to show love and devotion. However, it doesn't prove that persons with autism are distant and averse to forming bonds with others.

Chapter 4: Effective procedures for controlling the emotions of autistic children

There is a misconception that kids with autism have little or no emotions. The opposite is true in every way. Even while children with autism may have emotional outbursts for various causes or express their feelings in other ways, they still experience emotions just like everyone else.

Sometimes, children with autism may exhibit even more emotional sensitivity than some of their classmates. However, they could require assistance in expressing themselves if they have a hard time letting their emotions out.

It may be quite difficult to have high-functioning autism. On the one hand, you possess the linguistic and mental abilities to function in a conventional context. On the other side, you don't have the social, communication, or executive functioning abilities necessary to adapt successfully to change.

Bright lights, loud sounds, and high expectations may be almost hard for you to handle at the same time as you deal with sensory dysfunction, anxiety, or other problems.

Even high-functioning children with autism often act out when they are really irritated or upset. They could act in ways that astonish or startle others around them when they do. They could, for instance:

- Tears and screaming throughout the meltdown, like a much younger kid
- Run away from a challenging circumstance, perhaps placing oneself at risk
- Turn hostile or harsh against oneself
- Overreact to the situation and find it difficult to remain cool; be unable to absorb the reasoning that, in another circumstance, would allow them to remain calm;
- become too distraught to hear comforting advice
- Display self-stimulatory tendencies (hand flapping, etc.).

The Mood Will Pass

Remind yourself and your kid that sobbing stems from an emotion that will pass like a threatening cloud. Despite the feeling that the sky is falling, the sun will rise once again.

As soon as your kid starts to feel distressed, teach them to take a few calm, deep breaths. When they're not unhappy, practice this often. Do it with them. Tell them that both toddlers and adults experience emotional turmoil and that we all need to learn how to control our emotions.

There would be Meltdowns

Some meltdowns may be caused by your child's responses and their desire to learn how to cope with sensitivities and frustrations and moderate themselves; to find solace and support inside.

By offering your kid techniques for self-soothing or self-calming before continuing, you may aid in the development of their ability to cope with strong emotional responses. There are several approaches to take, and most of us develop our own over time.

For instance, some kids find that a little period of alone is therapeutic. Others find that talking with someone or temporarily shifting their focus might be helpful.

When Things Are Quiet, Learn

You may discuss with your youngster how to control their emotions during neutral moments when they are not disturbed. They may overcome their worry and irritation by learning to accept them, and they can do so with a little patience or by doing things slowly.

Regarding the most effective techniques for teaching your kid to calm down, you might consult with their instructors.

Cut It Off

You may occasionally stop a meltdown when you know one is coming by chatting with your kid ahead and asking them how they could prevent it this time. Even better, consider rewarding them for their efforts.

When your youngster successfully masters self-modulation, the increased sense of confidence will be its own reward for both you and them.

Routine makes humans happy. Everyone benefits from having a set routine in their lives, regardless of age, lifestyle, or background. As a result of their recurring patterns of behavior, interests, and activities, children with autism benefit the most from routines. A significant strategy for bringing stability and comfort into their life is the observance of a set schedule.

Numerous studies have shown the benefits of establishing a consistent daily schedule for your autistic kid, including increased independence and improved social-emotional wellbeing.

Daily habits can:

- Strengthen the bond between the caregiver and the kid
- Lessen the tension and power battles
- Boost collaboration
- Cultivate a true feeling of control over their day

- Establish a safe and comfortable atmosphere

Your autistic kid may develop order in their lives with the support of regularity and predictability.

Because of the following, routines are essential to their success:

It's Natural to Be Routine

Autism-related children often favor monotony and repetition. Routines are second nature to them, whether for their favorite pursuits, pastimes, meals, or bedtimes. Routines may be a fantastic tool for assisting your kids in a manner that comes naturally and comforts them.

Routine Helps Reduce Stress

Knowing what to anticipate at any given moment in their routine may be a source of relaxation for everyone, even kids with autism. A schedule may aid your kid as they learn to successfully navigate their lives as they grow to understand their surroundings and expectations. Children with autism often struggle to make sense of novel noises, actions, or experiences. Routine brings order to an otherwise chaotic world. By teaching them what to anticipate, when to expect it, and how to respond, a routine may help people live more orderly lives. Your kid may flourish if you are predictable.

Routine Can Benefit Autism Children Learn new abilities

They're more open to learning new skills and honing their current ones when they feel comfortable, secure, and less stressed. By giving kids a routine they are used to, you may not only help them deal with potentially stressful circumstances but also position them to succeed in new endeavors.

TIPS FOR MAINTAINING A ROUTINE SUCCESSFULLY

It need not be difficult or burdensome to establish an effective routine for your kid. Create a routine that benefits the entire family by using the advice in the following list:

- To assist your youngster to comprehend their schedule, use a visual aid like a calendar for the refrigerator or a poster for the wall.
- Use tools like a sticker system and positive reinforcement to encourage work completion.
- Keep referring back to the visual timetable and stress how important each activity or event is.
- Before, during, and after each assignment, talk to your kid to explain what is happening.

Once you and your kid have established a pattern, gradually include new activities to teach them new abilities and habits.

You must provide your kid the resources and abilities necessary to flourish if you are parenting a child with autism. Creating and upholding routines will go a long way toward assisting your kid in developing new abilities, moving forward, and accomplishing objectives.

Here are some suggestions for teaching your ASD kid to control their emotions, but it's crucial to stress that your child must first be able to recognize and categorize different emotions. Before going on to the next, complete each of these stages by comprehending it and doing it.

Step1 :Create a chart of feelings as your first step.

You may make a visual tool that illustrates the many emotional states that a youngster could experience as they go from satisfaction to rage using the now-common emojis. The youngster may choose their own categories and give each emotion a name that corresponds to their own emotions. You can put images of the emotions in one column of a chart—possibly on a dry-erase board or any board with sticky notes—and have the child fill in examples of those situations in the second column, which is labeled "this is how I feel when" to describe how they feel in that particular circumstance.

Step 2: Use symbols or language to represent each level.

The more the youngster is exposed to the emotions, the more likely they are to identify them for themselves by using their own names and descriptions for the chart. By asking your kid to answer questions about these sensations, you may assist them. You may ask them to finish the sentence "I feel pleased when..." at each emotional image at each level, for instance. If the kid is unresponsive to these suggestions, you may ask the child to apply an emotional reaction to a situation you have just described and to check that it matches the images on the child's chart.

Step 3: Explain acceptable emotions with the use of examples.

Once you and your kid have experienced some of the scenarios on the chart, you may talk about concrete instances of how to calmly recognize how to prevent emotions from rising to the next higher degree of rage or fear. For instance, if your child is extremely upset because he can't read his favorite book one night, you could point out that while that is a disappointing fact, the more appropriate perspective in that situation would be in the "slightly upset" row rather than the "intensely angry" category. You could then use another example of what would instead fall in the "intensely angry" row as a comparison. Don't build a mountain out of a molehill, the proverb says about keeping things in perspective.

Step 4: Explain and show improved coping techniques

You may show your kid how to prevent being "extremely upset" by teaching them coping mechanisms when they become aware that they are about to experience the initial sense of being "a little disturbed" by employing role-playing. With time and effort, the youngster will be able to recognize the coping mechanism that is most appropriate in each situation.

Step 5: Practice the "what if" scenario.

If you can think of an instance that might challenge your kid's capacity for emotional control, articulate it, ask your child to do the same, and then discuss with them in a relaxed context what they may do if such an instance occurred in real life. Remind your youngster that they have overcome far more trying circumstances in the past and that it's equally vital to take lessons from previous experiences and then let go of those bad feelings after they've overcome them.

Step 6: If you wish to teach the same thing, be composed and patient.

You could find it simple to climb the mountain by yourself in these scenarios, which might be emotionally fraught for everyone concerned. To assist your kid climb down the mountain during a rising fear, try to prepare yourself beforehand by formulating a strategy and keeping a list of reminders with step-by-step instructions. It may be useful to have that list available to use in case a circumstance similar to this one occurs. Always keep in mind that you are setting an example.

Chapter 5: Acknowledging and Helping your child.

A diagnosis of ASD may be especially terrifying since no parent is ever ready to learn that their kid is anything other than happy and healthy. You could be perplexed by contradictory treatment recommendations or unaware of how to best assist your kid. You could also be afraid that nothing you do will change since you've been informed that ASD is an incurable, lifelong disorder.

Even while it's true that ASD isn't something a person just "grows out of," there are several therapies that may assist kids in learning new abilities and overcoming a broad range of developmental obstacles. To fulfill your child's specific needs and enable them to learn, develop, and flourish in life, support is available, including free government services, in-home behavioral treatment, and school-based programs.

It's crucial to look for oneself when caring for a kid with autism. Being emotionally resilient enables you to provide the greatest care possible for your kid.

These parenting hints may ease the burden of raising a kid who has autism.

- Stop waiting for a diagnosis.

The greatest thing you can do as a parent of a kid with ASD or associated developmental delays is to begin therapy as soon as possible. As soon as you suspect a problem, get assistance. Don't hold off to see whether your youngster will eventually catch up or outgrow the issue. Waiting for a formal diagnosis is unnecessary. The better the possibility of treatment success for children with autism spectrum conditions, the sooner they get assistance. The best strategy to accelerate a child's growth and lessen autism symptoms over time is via early intervention.

- Study up on autism.

The more knowledgeable you are about autism spectrum conditions, the more able you will be to make choices for your kid. Ask questions, get knowledgeable about the available treatments, and take part in choosing your own therapy.

- Gain expertise in your kid.

Find out what causes your child's difficult or disruptive behaviors and what makes them go away. What frightens or stresses out your child? Calming? Uncomfortable? Enjoyable? Understanding how your kid is affected can help you solve issues more effectively and avoid or alter challenging circumstances.

- Embrace your child's differences.

Practice acceptance rather than concentrating on how your autistic child differs from other kids and what he or she is "missing." Enjoy your child's unique traits, acknowledge tiny victories, and refrain from comparing your child to others. More than anything else, your kid will benefit from feeling welcomed and loved unconditionally.

- Never give up.

The trajectory of autism spectrum conditions cannot be predicted. Don't assume anything about how your child's life will turn out. People with autism have a lifetime to mature and hone their skills, just like everyone else.

Fostering your autistic child's development

1.Establish boundaries and security

Your kid will benefit greatly from your involvement in therapy and your efforts to learn as much as you can about autism. The following advice can also help you and your kid with ASD live more comfortably at home:

- Be dependable. Children with ASD struggle to transfer their knowledge from one environment, like the classroom or therapist's office, to another, like their home. For instance, your kid could communicate with you at home using sign language, but not at school. The most effective strategy to support learning is to provide stability in your child's surroundings. Learn what the therapists are doing with your kid and use the same methods at home. To help your kid apply what he or she has learned from one setting to another, consider having treatment take place in more than one location. It's crucial to maintain consistency in how you speak to your kid and handle difficult behaviors.

- Follow a timetable. Children with autism often do better when they follow a routine or timetable that is very regimented. This relates once again to the constancy they both need and want. Establish a routine for your child's meals, therapy sessions, school hours, and sleep. Try to limit the number of times this process is interrupted. If a schedule change is inevitable, have your youngster ready for it in advance.

- Reward excellent conduct. With children with ASD, positive reinforcement may go a long way, so try to "catch them doing something nice." Be extremely explicit about the conduct you're praising them for when you congratulate them when they behave correctly or when they master a new ability. Consider other methods of rewarding them for excellent conduct, such as letting them play with a favorite item or giving them a sticker.

- Make your house a safe place. Create a personal area in your house where your youngster may unwind, feel comfortable, and feel secure. This calls for structuring and establishing limits in a manner that your youngster can comprehend. Visual clues may be useful (colored tape marking areas that are off limits, labeling items in the house with pictures). Additionally, you may want to safety-proof your home, especially if your kid is prone to tantrums or other self-harming behaviors.

2. Look for nonverbal cues to communicate.
It may be difficult to connect with a kid who has autism, but you don't need to speak to them or even touch them to do so. Your body language, tone of voice, how you look at your kid, and sometimes even how you touch them are all ways that you can connect with them. Even if your kid never talks, they are talking with you anyway. All you have to do is study the language.

- Observe any nonverbal indications. You may learn to recognize the nonverbal clues that autistic children use to communicate if you are attentive and aware. When a person is weary, hungry, or in need of anything, you may tell by the noises they make, their facial expressions, and the actions they make.

- Determine the cause of the temper tantrum. When you are misunderstood or disregarded, it's only normal to feel sad, and this is also true for children with ASD. Children with ASD often act out when you fail to notice their nonverbal signs, according to research. Their method of expressing their annoyance and demanding your attention is through tantruming.

- Schedule an enjoyable time. Despite having ASD, a kid is still a child. There must be more to life than treatment for parents and children with autism. Decide when your kid will be most awake and attentive for fun. Consider the things that make your kid laugh, smile, and come out of her/his shell as you try to come up with methods to have fun together. If these activities don't appear therapeutic or instructional, your youngster is most likely to enjoy them. Both you and your kid will gain a lot by taking pleasure in one another's presence and spending time together unhurriedly. All children need to play to learn, and it shouldn't seem like work.

- Keep an eye out for your child's sensory needs. Many kids with ASD have extreme sensitivity to touch, sound, light, smell, and taste. Some autistic children exhibit "under-sensitivity" to sensory stimuli. Analyze your child's "bad" or disruptive actions to see what sights, sounds, scents, movements, and tactile sensations they are drawn to, as well as what makes them feel good. What causes stress in your child? Calming? Uncomfortable? Enjoyable? You'll be more adept at solving issues, avoiding sticky situations, and fostering positive experiences if you know what impacts your kid.

3. Make a specialized autism treatment strategy

It might be difficult to decide which therapy is best for your kid when there are so many options available. You can get various or even contradicting advice from your parents, professors, and physicians, further complicating the situation.

Remember that no one therapy is effective for everyone when creating a treatment plan for your kid. Every autistic individual is distinct, with their own unique talents and shortcomings.

The course of therapy for your kid should be personalized for their particular need. It is up to you to see that their needs are satisfied since you are the one who knows your kid the best.

You may achieve it by asking the following questions yourself:

1. What are the advantages and disadvantages of my child?
2. Which actions are the most problematic?
3. What crucial abilities does my kid lack?
4. Which kind of learning is better for my child: watching, listening, or doing?
5. What activities does my kid want to perform, and how can we utilize them in therapy and support learning?

Finally, remember that your participation is essential to the success of any treatment strategy, regardless of the one selected. By collaborating with the treatment team and completing the therapy at home, you can ensure that your kid gets the most out of their treatment. (This is why it's crucial to prioritize your health!)

4. Look for aid and assistance

Taking care of a kid with autism may take a lot of time and effort. There may be times when you feel anxious, disheartened, or overburdened. Raising a kid with special needs is significantly harder than parenting a typical youngster. You must look after yourself if you want to be the best parent you can be.

Don't attempt to do everything by yourself. You're not required to! Families of children with ASD have a variety of resources at their disposal for guidance, assistance, advocacy, and support:

- ASD support groups - Getting involved in an ASD support group is a terrific opportunity to connect with other families going through similar struggles. Parents may rely on one another for emotional support, information sharing, and guidance. The loneliness many parents face after learning their kid has a diagnosis may sometimes be much diminished by just being with others who are in the same situation and listening to their stories.

- Counseling for individuals, couples, or families - You may wish to consult your own therapist if stress, anxiety, or depression are starting to affect you. Therapy is a secure setting where you may openly discuss all of your feelings, good, terrible, and ugly. Marriage and family counseling may also assist you in resolving issues that the difficulties of raising an autistic kid are producing in your marriage or with other family members.

Know the rights of your kid

You have the following legal rights as the parent of a kid with ASD:

- Participate in the whole IEP process for your kid.
- disagree with the suggestions of the educational system
- Get your youngster evaluated by a third party.
- You may ask anybody you wish to be a part of the IEP team, from a family to your child's doctor.
- If you think your child's needs are not being fulfilled, you may request an IEP meeting at any time.
- If you can't reach a compromise with the school,
- you may get free or inexpensive legal assistance

Finally, as ASD parents it is important to take some time to yourself by following this helpful tips:

1. Ensure your own well-being.

You must maintain peak physical and mental health as a caregiver to be able to handle the obstacles that arise daily. This calls for taking your time and finding methods to look after yourself so that you have enough of yourself (physically, psychologically, and emotionally) to share.

ASD parents often experience higher levels of stress than parents of children with other disorders. Caretakers may experience relationship breakdowns and even psychiatric problems if the problem is not addressed. Your health might also be impacted by stress. Keep your affairs to keep from being overburdened. This entails setting aside time each day for oneself. Among the crucial and even enjoyable methods to achieve it are:

2. Determine the true origins of your stress. If you're feeling overwhelmed, divide your main problems into smaller, more manageable portions. You'll have a strategy and feel better.

Other options include meditation. Be mindful of your inner dialogue as much as your ideas. You'll be able to eliminate pointless concerns.

3. Exercise.

You are not required to visit the gym. Swim, exercise in the yard, dance in the kitchen, or just go for a walk. These are quick and efficient methods to work out.

Take an exercise class if you want some adult companionship. It's a fantastic way to make new friends and get your energy back.

4. Go to sleep.

There is no substitute for a restful night's sleep when it comes to rejuvenating your body and mind. Use meditation or relaxation techniques to aid in your relaxation if necessary. That might aid in getting your body ready for sleep.

5. Be inventive with your cuisine.

You probably put a lot of effort into making sure your kid eats well-balanced meals. How are you doing? Consider experimenting with new fruits, vegetables, and cuisines to spice up your unique food. To keep things fresh, look for new recipes. and adhere to a daily eating routine. You can keep your system on track and your energy levels up.

6.Get your life in order.

This is the secret to overcoming obstacles in life while maintaining a good standard of living. You and your family will all gain. Schedule some time each week for mingling and having fun. To bring balance to your hectic days, try these suggestions:

7.Locate your pals.

You do really have a kid with special needs. But you are also a person. Being aware of your own individuality helps you be a better parent. Spend some time laughing and reuniting with your buddies. You'll be happy that you did.

8.Rekindle previous interests.
Find your knitting needles, clean the piano, or take the golf clubs out of the bag. Try out some new hobbies that interest you.

9.Count to five each day.
Spending a few additional minutes in the morning may help you focus and set the tone for the rest of the day.

10.Consider taking a long, warm shower, gathering your thoughts, or writing down some ideas in a diary.
Do it quickly. Can your spouse or other family members temporarily take up the role of parent? You may get some much-needed alone time by taking a simple stroll around the block or a short trip to the shop.

www.ingramcontent.com/pod-product-compliance
Lightning Source LLC
LaVergne TN
LVHW020526160826
845677LV00015B/3932
* 9 7 9 8 8 4 7 8 9 5 7 9 8 *